"WHAT IF"

... you have a stroke or dementia,

... your child has Special Needs,

... the unexpected happens.

Is Your Family protected?"

Martha Jo Geisler Patterson, J.D., CELA*

Published by RCP Publications

*certified by the National Elder Law Foundation

Published by Geisler Patterson Law
Burbank, CA 91510
www.ElderLawMom.com

Copyright 2016© Geisler Patterson Law. All Rights Reserved.

The information contained in this book is not, nor is it intended to be, legal advice. You should contact an attorney directly for advice concerning your individual situation and needs. The information contained in the book is factual at the time of publication, but cannot be guaranteed to be accurate at later dates.

No part of this book can be quoted, paraphrased, cited, presented, recorded, or otherwise utilized without permission of the publisher. No part of the book may be stored, recorded, or otherwise placed in a retrieval system, nor transmitted, or reproduced in any way, including, but not limited to, digital copying or printing, without the prior written permission of the publisher.

Table of Contents

My Story	1
Part 1 What is Estate Planning and Why is it important?	6
Part 2 Why Estate Planning is not as Simple as it seems	8
Part 3 What if You …Die or become disabled	11
Part 4 Lessons learned from a Failed Trust	14
Part 5 What is a Trust? Do I need One?	17
Part 6 Old trust, no trust, wrong trust? Could Your trust fail?	21
Part 7 Different Trusts, Different Purposes	26
Part 8 Do I Really Need To Do A Special Kind Of Trust For My Disabled Child?	29
Part 9 What happens if you lose your mind?	32
Part 10 What is a Power of Attorney for Finances, Why do I need it?	36
Part 11 Health Care Decisions, how can someone help?	40
Part 12 Paying for Care in a Nursing Home	50
Part 13 Veteran's Benefits, Annuities, and Accreditation	53
Part 14 Veteran's Benefits to Pay for Care	55
Part 15 Nine Common And Costly Estate Planning Mistakes	59
Part 16 "Now What"	64

My story

My first real job (after working at Disneyland) was working as a Supervisor in a program helping adults with disabilities get training to work at Beckman Industries. I loved the people I worked with, but wanted to do more to help people. I decided to go to law school, and wanted to be a litigator. After earning my law degree, I spent the first ten years of my practice as a successful litigator, winning a number of cases. Over time, however, I realized that while litigation can be fun for the lawyers, money is the only remedy for damage, whether for abuse, an accident, or worse. I wanted to use my law degree to assist people in other ways. My children were young then, so I left a mid-size litigation firm to start my own.

I was truly impressed by the mentors I met through NAELA (National Academy of Elder Law Attorneys). Several elder law attorneys in particular provided invaluable counsel and inspiration: Fay Blix, Donna Bashaw, and Betsy Angevine are among the women who mentored and encouraged me, along with the late Cliffton Kruse, whose writings showed me that you can be a lawyer who cares about clients and makes a difference in the world.

I have become so passionate about helping the elderly and those with disabilities that I have become one of less than 35 attorneys in California to be certified as an Elder Law Attorney. I am very proud of the fact that I have not only passed a rigorous exam, but also have served enough people in the past years to meet the experience criterion for the Certification

My Greatest Source Of Inspiration? My Parents
My father, Joseph Brokaw Geisler, was City Attorney of Anaheim. He died of lung cancer when I was in high school, ten months after we lost my dear brother in an auto accident. I am now older than my father was when he died, and I doubt I will ever accomplish as much as he did in his short life. He served in World War II and earned two Navy Crosses and the Distinguished Flying Star for his bravery. As City Attorney, he brought the Anaheim Stadium and the Anaheim Convention center to reality. He was known as a man who told you what you needed to know, not what you wanted to hear. I still remember when he received death threats for allowing the Hells Angels to hold a funeral procession down the

main street of Anaheim, and how he became friends with Dr. Ralph Wilkerson because he did not allow the Walt Disney Company to forbid the Melodyland Theater from becoming a church across the street from Disneyland park. I hope I will always maintain my integrity as my father did; and that I will always tell my clients what they need to hear, not what they want to hear.

My mother is 89, and remains the most amazing woman I know. She lives at home despite many illnesses. After my father died, she went back to work. She had the tenacity to learn how to operate the Mag Card II electronic typewriter, for at that time, it was a highly desired skill among employers. She worked for the City of Anaheim, retired, and then worked for Poe's Plumbing to complete her Social Security quarters. She has lived a frugal life and invested well thanks to her good friend Douglas Ogden. She has generously paid for my children to attend private Christian Schools. I have been able to make sure that my mother has a Trust that protects her while she is alive, and which will protect her child and grandchildren when she dies. She was wise enough to purchase Long Term Care Insurance through

PERS when the City of Anaheim offered it. Her health is failing, and I am glad that she will have this resource so she can stay at home.

I have helped hundreds of families with planning for what happens when you die and what happens when you don't die but live with dementia, disability, or disease. I have spent over a thousand hours studying the laws related to Wills, Trusts, and Powers of Attorney, Health Care Directives, Medi-Cal Planning, Veteran's Benefits and Special Needs Trusts. I have read countless articles about Alzheimer's, Dementia, various diseases, and disabilities. I saw the signs as my mother in-law started forgetting things, and I knew that she and her husband would need help. Yet despite all my education, experience and knowledge I have learned many things from the journey our family is taking with her.

In this book I will be sharing things I am learning on my journey as a caregiver who is part of the sandwich generation, caring for parents and children at the same time. My goal is to provide you with a guide to help you on your journey.

Part One

What is Estate Planning and Why is it important

You have worked hard; you should want to protect your family. Estate Planning is giving what you have, to whom you want, the way you want with the least taxes and fees possible.

My goal is to help everyone who comes in my office to achieve that goal.

It's taken years of hard work to get where you are today. Now you want to protect your assets for your enjoyment and that of your loved ones; maintain control of your affairs should you become incapacitated; and ensure that your wishes will be carried out after you are gone. Chances are, you have a number of questions about how to accomplish these goals, including:
- What do I need to do to control my property during my lifetime?
- How can I leave the most to my children, grandchildren, and loved ones without losing control of my assets?

- How do I eliminate or minimize income, gift, estate and capital gains taxes?
- What are the best ways to protect and preserve my assets?
- What is the best way to protect my real estate investments?
- How do I protect my children and loved ones from losing their inheritances to predators, creditors, family disharmony, or even their own poor decisions?
- Will I outlive my money if I need nursing home or assisted living care?
- Do I need long term care insurance?

The answers to these and other questions can only be answered on an individual basis, by an attorney like me whose practice is concentrated on estate planning and asset protection planning as well as specializing in elder law. I hope that this book will be a tool and guide to help you along in beginning to answer some of these questions.

Part Two

Why Estate Planning is not as Simple as it seems

This Could Happen To You

     Bob's parents and little brother are killed in an automobile crash. Mom had filled out a form so a "cheap" legal service would prepare wills for her and her husband. Somehow, they were never signed, and those unsigned wills named Mom's best friend as the guardian. Best friend convinced everyone she should be the one to take care of Bob. As soon as the life insurance policy and the automobile policy were part of Bob's estate, it was apparent that the best friend was only interested in the money. A painful guardianship battle ensued. It was clear that Dad had never liked Mom's best friend, and that the wills would have named a family member if only this family had met with an attorney. **Guardianships are essential.**

A couple just starting out with two children at home creates their own wills, using an Internet service. They leave everything to each other, and then to their children. Unfortunately, one dies of cancer, and the other dies in a work related accident. The probate court is forced to require annual accountings and appearances. Much of their children's inheritance is paid to lawyers. When each child turns 18, they receive what is left. $600,000.00 is too much for any 18 years old to handle. **A simple will is not enough.**

Grace's husband passes away; all the property is immediately hers because it was in joint tenancy. Her children quickly realize her memory is failing. She is not paying her bills or taking her medications. Dirk, her drug addict son, convinces her he is now clean and sober, and is the only child who loves her. He moves in, never lets her answer the phone, or allows his brothers or sisters to visit. He spends all moms' money on himself, uses her credit cards, and even gets new ones in his name. The other children finally go to Court, they paid the attorney's fees. Mom is left with no money, and has suffered from malnutrition. **You need to protect your money while you are alive.**

Anne was widowed when her children were in High School. It took a long time but she finally found a job. She was able to help her children go to College. She wanted to make sure that her children would have something when she was gone. She prudently purchased life insurance. Her son married a very wise and prudent woman, but her daughter married a man who loved expensive toys (plasma T.V., sports cars, and expensive wine). Anne was blessed with four grandchildren from her daughter. Anne was saving up money to help pay for her grand-children's education. She passed away before her oldest grandchild graduated from High School. Her estate passed easily to her two children through her living trust. Her daughter spent the inheritance she received on toys for her husband. When her daughter's children were ready for college there was no money left to pay for it. **You may want an inheritance protection trust to protect your children or grandchildren.**

Part Three

What if You ... Die or become Disabled

What if...? I know you don't want to think about it, and yet I know you do. You worry and worry. When I sit with a family we talk about "what if". Planning for what if is the most important thing any family can do. I have lived through many what ifs. How many what ifs have you lived through?

Have you planned for what ifs? What if you die? What if you are disabled and unable to take care of yourself? What if you have dementia? These are questions you don't want to ask. Procrastination is the most common estate planning mistake. We all want to put off thinking of bad things; we hope if we ignore them they will go away. Of course when death, disability, or dementia hit your home if you aren't ready the only option is Court. The Court proceedings related to death, disability and death are expensive and humiliating. Avoiding Court requires planning.

You may be surprised that 80% of all Trusts fail: they fail to avoid probate, fail to plan for disability or to avoid

Conservatorship, and fail to avoid the loss of inheritances to creditors and predators and divorce. Why do Trusts fail? The law changes and as the law changes your Trust needs to be changed. Families change, most families realize the importance of protecting an inheritance from creditors, predators and divorce. Circumstances change, families sense a loved one's memory is failing or realize that a child will always need help. Very few Trusts contain any plan for dementia or disability. It is six times more likely that you will become disabled this year than that you will die. Will your family be able to take care of you if you are unable to care for yourself? Is your Trust out of date?

If you don't come home what will happen to your children? Who will be their guardian? Will they lose their inheritance to creditors, predators or divorce? What about your spouse? Will your spouse remarry? If your spouse remarries everything you worked for might go to the new wife or husband. What if you are disabled? Who will take care of you? I have a guide with the 12 critical issues every estate plan should cover. If you want to find out if your trust is drafted properly, or stop procrastinating so your family has the peace of mind knowing they are prepared when bad things happen you should have your Trust reviewed, you can call (855) ELDER77 or (855)353-3777 and if you mention this chapter I review your Trust at no charge. Later in this book I will discuss why Trusts fail.

Part Four

Lessons learned from a Failed Trust

For several years, my husband, together with his brother and sister-in-law, had discussed their concern about my mother-in-law. She did not seem to be doing well. She was forgetting things, yet she denied that her memory was failing. My dear father-in-law did everything he could to protect her dignity and cover for the memory loss, so we did not know how bad things were until my father in-law fell and broke his hip. Like many people with Dementia or Alzheimer's Disease, the severity of the memory loss is not apparent until some part of the fragile structure that enables them to function falls apart. My father-in-law's injury was such an event. It became immediately apparent that my mother-in law could not be left alone, could not pay the bills and could not care for her very modest estate.

At the time, my in-laws knew I was extremely busy with my career and my children. They did not want to burden me further, and as they were out of town, had their Living Trust created by another attorney. Eventually, the family needed to review this trust. I became involved, but nobody could find the original, or even a copy. Finally, we found a business card, and I contacted their Estate Attorney. He provided me with copies, for a charge of $230.00. Part of my inspiration for creating my Trust Loving Care (TLC) maintenance program is based on the trauma we all suffered when we did not know who did the Trust and where it was, as well as our resentment about having to pay for the copies. All of my clients are offered the opportunity each year to invite their Trustees to meet with me, and when they join the TLC program, their family is never charged for a copy of the Trust, or the call to me when their loved one passes away-and they, like my husband and brother, need to know what to do.

I wish I could say that the stress associated with this event ended with finding the attorney and getting a copy of the Trust. It did not. The Trust itself failed. Why? The Trust was ten years old, and the successor Trustee was my father-in-law's best friend, who at 82 was just not able to do the job. My mother in-law could not change the Trust since it was obvious she lacked the capacity to make legal decisions. Yet she believed that she was fine and did not want to see a doctor about her condition. We spoke to her primary care physician, who was more than willing to verify that she lacked capacity, but HIPAA prevented him from talking to another doctor, and like ALMOST EVERY TRUST NOT DRAFTED BY AN ELDER LAW ATTORNEY, this trust required two doctors to sign that she did not have capacity. So, despite the fact that it was obvious, we could not do anything unless we could get her to a doctor, and you cannot legally make someone go to a doctor. We ended up having to obtain a Conservatorship of her person, and moved her to a Secured Memory Facility. When my father-in law passed away, and the Power of Attorney my brother-in law used to pay bills was no longer valid, the Trust failed again. Why? The bank had misinformed us, and their CD was not in the Trust, so we now are required to account for her money in Conservatorship Probate Court. All of this could have been avoided. Having seen firsthand the catastrophic results of inadequate planning, I am fully committed to making sure that my clients, and their families, will not have to go through what my family and I did.

Part Five

What is a Trust? Do I need One?

A Trust is a legal document, a contract between the person who makes the Trust (the Grantor or Settlor), and the Trustee and Successor Trustees. The Trustee and the Grantor can be the same person. A Trust works like a wagon. If you put your toys in the wagon, and pull it away, the wagon and the toys go together. The toys that aren't in the wagon stay where they are. The person who has the ability to pull the wagon is the person who decides where the wagon goes and what happens to the toys in the wagon. A trust only controls assets that are put in the trust. If an asset is not transferred into the Trust then the asset is not controlled by the Trust. One of the jobs of the Estate Planning or Elder Law Attorney is to help you make sure that all your assets are in your trust and that any assets that are not in your trust have been left out by design and that there is a plan for those assets too.

Here are some questions about Wills and Trusts that I am often asked:

Q.   What is the difference between a Will and a Trust?

A.   A Will takes effect after you pass away. Generally, if your estate is over $150,000 and if you have a Will your estate may have to go through Probate. There are many types of trusts. A Living Trust is the type of Trust that most people have. Most Living Trusts are only designed to avoid probate, our office provides you with more options. In our office you will be provided with options that will enable you to truly protect your family. Our trusts plan for life, and protect your spouse, children and grandchildren from creditors and predators. If you have a Trust and have transferred your assets to the Trust, then your estate will not have to go through Probate.

Q.   What is Probate?

A.   Probate is a court process. Generally, there are several steps to the probate process. The court appoints a person to be in charge of the decedent's estate. This person is called the personal representative or executor.

The personal representative gathers the decedent's assets; pays the decedent's appropriate bills; he or she may sell certain of the decedent's assets; files tax returns; and distributes the decedent's assets to the appropriate persons or entities. All of this is done under the court's supervision. In Probate both the attorney and the executor each receive fees set by statute, these fees can be very expensive, and with the fee set at 4% of the first $100,000.00 and 3% of the next $100,000.00 and 2% of the next $800,000.00, and attorneys are allowed to ask for extraordinary fees.

Q. Why do people want to avoid Probate?

A. Probate has become a bad word in our society. It can be a time consuming and costly process. Proper estate planning can avoid Probate. If you do need to go through the Probate process, our office can help you through every step of the process.

Q. What happens if I die without a Will?

A. In California, if you die without a Will, the State of California and the Superior Court will decide who will be in charge of your estate and who will inherit your estate.

So do you NEED a Trust?

I'm a lawyer, so my answer to almost every question is IT DEPENDS!

Most people want to avoid probate, since probate can take long and is expensive. A Trust easily avoids probate and can save a family thousands of dollars. For most families a Trust avoids court. However, in the past twenty years Trust litigation has exploded, and Trust litigation can be more time consuming and expensive than a Probate. If you have a family prone to fight and sue, or a step family situation you should spend time considering the options with litigation in mind.

Whatever you do, you need a plan.

Part Six

Old trust, no trust, wrong trust? Could your trust fail?

Many people who come into my office already have trusts. On average the Trusts brought into my office are about ten years old. Laws change, families change, and you change. A Trust should be reviewed every three to five years to make sure that it incorporates the most recent laws. Some changes in the law have little effect on existing trusts, others like the major changes in the laws related to estate taxes or the rules related to obtaining assistance from Veteran's Benefits or Medicaid (in California we call the program Medi-Cal) can affect everyone, even those with small estates.

Changes in the laws will affect the recommendations competent attorneys make to their clients. A trust which is a perfect solution for a family can be the wrong solution when laws change. For instance when I became a lawyer, Estate Taxes were charged to estates larger than $650,000.00. Lawyers planning Estates prior to the law changing made sure that the first person to die would use up their Estate Tax Exemption, which would allow the second to die to have $650,000 as their tax exemption. This was the planning most families needed. The down side is that when the first spouse died part of the assets stayed in the Trust, and two tax returns were needed. A further downside is that if the surviving spouse needs care in a Nursing Home the part set aside must be used for care before the person can qualify for Medi-Cal. Sadly, I know many widows who lost a spouse, and have this kind of Trust; when their spouse died they had about $750,000 in assets, today they have around the same amount and not only do not need the cumbersome trusts to avoid estate taxes, they also end up unable to save the money and get help from Medi-Cal to pay for the high cost of medical care.

It is extremely important that when your family changes due to death or divorce that you revise your Trust. A major family change will change how you want your assets distributed. A divorce changes what you own, and for most people when they divorce they no longer wish their (former) spouse to receive all their assets when they die. If a child dies before a parent, this could change who you want to receive your assets when you die. In the event of the death of a child, you should have your Trust reviewed since even if you are sure that your assets will go to the right person. If your memory or health is failing, your Trust needs to be updated. In this situation it is extremely important that you have a plan. The sickest person is not always the person who passes first. The Alzheimer's association has found that 80% of caregivers die first. Most people are just like my in-laws, they have sweetheart Trusts (if I die my sweet-heart takes over); this is great when your sweetheart is well, but if they are suffering from dementia or a disabling disease they will not be able to take over. Unless you have planned for an easy transition when the caregiver spouse dies there will be difficulty. Your loved one may like my mother in-law be so distraught and confused that they do not trust anyone and will not allow anyone to take over, or they just may want to hold on to the job desperately wanting to keep what little control over their life that remains. Either way it is easier to deal with these issues while the caregiver is alive.

If you have no Trust, you are guaranteed Probate (average cost $25,000). No Trust guarantees when your memory fails and you can't remember to pay your bills; you will be under Conservatorship, the court proceeding to allow someone to care for you and your money while you are alive (average cost over $100,000). No Trust, no Will and no Plan: your assets will go to whomever the law dictates; someone you love may be left out. A Trust may not be the best option for you, but you do need a plan and a way for someone to legally handle your affairs. Ironically, if you are in the unfortunate situation where you don't have anyone you trust then you should plan all your affairs so that the Court WILL supervise them if you lose the ability to handle your own money, or when you or your loved one dies. Court may be expensive, but it is less expensive than losing everything to someone who steals your money. Sadly, I have lost count of all the stories I have heard, and all the Court cases I have seen or been involved in where the untrustworthy relatives have stolen everything leaving the elderly victim with no money to use to go after the thief. Sadly, the police and District Attorneys are rarely able to prosecute these crimes.

In my next chapter I will discuss the different kinds of Trusts. If you or a loved one uses Medi-Cal to pay for medical or nursing home care, the state will require that you pay back every dime spent. The State can and will require the beneficiaries of a "Living Trust", and wills to pay it all back from the estate. If a loved one is in a skilled nursing home a special "Medi-Cal" Trust can protect all the assets from the State. Medi-Cal planning can save thousands of dollars. Veterans can use a trust similar to the "Medi-Cal" Trust to qualify for Aid and Attendance benefits. If a loved one is disabled, a "Special Needs Trust" is necessary to provide maximum care, while not causing the loved one to lose valuable benefits.

Part Seven

Different Trusts, Different Purposes

I mentioned that there are different kinds of Trusts, and there are many different kinds of Trusts each with a specific purpose. There are trusts specifically designed to avoid Estate and Capital Gains taxes allowing those with millions of dollars to pass money while minimizing all the taxes which apply to larger estates. There are Trusts designed to give money to Charities, and there are Trusts designed to care for pets. Each of these trusts has its place; I routinely have helped families with this kind of planning. However the focus of what I do is to help middle class families with planning to pay for care. The Trusts I use most often are my Medi-Cal Compliant Asset Protection Trust, my Veteran Benefits Compliant Asset Protection Trust, my Medi-Cal and Veteran's Benefits Compliant Asset Protection Trust, and my Special Needs Trust.

The most frequent question I am asked is "I have a Trust, Why do I need a new one?" This is a really good question. The answer I usually give is the traditional Living Trust is a revocable Trust and all the assets are available to pay for care now and available to pay back the State of California for any benefits received. Living Trusts are open boxes everything is available; if you need help paying for care, your Living Trust does nothing to help you. You will need a trust designed especially for this purpose, an Asset Protection Trust that protects your assets and enables you to get the help you need.

Medi-Cal and the Veteran's Administration have rules; their rules are not the same, but there are similarities in the programs. The main similarity is that both programs require low assets. The other similarity is that planning for one can require planning for the other, so the it requires special knowledge that people like me who spend a lot of time on these matters and become Certified as Elder Law Attorneys know. When you know the rules you know how to plan. The special Trusts I create comply with the rules set out by Medi-Cal and/or the Veteran's Administration so that people can get the assistance they need and retain most of their assets. A Special Needs Trust is designed especially for a person who will receive an inheritance and who needs to maintain their eligibility for benefits available to people with disabilities, or for those who have a special need for protection.

Unfortunately, for most regular folks, all of this is confusing. The documents look the same, and there are even ads saying "You don't need a lawyer to do a Living Trust"; well I won't say the ads are a lie, but the truth is you need a lawyer to tell you what you need, and most people do not know enough about trusts to know if their do it yourself document is adequate to meet their needs. I don't need a mechanic to change my oil, but I do need a mechanic to look at my car and tell me if everything on my car is okay and that I don't need to repair anything.

Part Eight

Do I Really Need To Do A Special Kind Of Trust For My Disabled Child?

The Wall Street Journal ran an article on October 9, 2008, "An Estate Plan Built for Special Needs"; and many of my clients and friends called me to tell me that the Wall Street Journal was saying exactly what I had been telling them! I am passionate about planning specifically for disabled children.

It is very sad when a disabled child outlives their parents. Parents are unique; they love their child unconditionally and care for them regardless of the challenge. This is particularly true of mothers. Women typically bear the burden of care for both their parents and their children. A disabled child continues to need their mother (and father) long after most children are caring for their own parents.

An Estate Plan for a "Special Needs Child" must be designed to maximize the public benefits available to provide medical care, and a stipend for food and shelter, providing funds for everything else. The first Special

Needs Trust I ever did was for a lovely lady who had a son with Down Syndrome; she had cancer, and he still lived at home. We were able to plan so he could continue to live at home, while receiving a check from SSI. His medical care, which was extensive, was covered by Medicare and Medi-Cal, and her best friend who was the Trustee could make sure that the videos he loved were rented for him, and he had the comic books he loved so much.

The rules for these Trusts are rather complicated. Most attorneys do not understand this area of Law, and believe that all you need to do is put in the right words. The right words are indeed critical, as a Trust for Special Needs should have instructions so the Trustee knows what things the person loves, so that the comic books and videos and other pleasures of life are provided.

Grandparents, aunts and uncles who want to help by providing for the disabled person must make sure that they have an Estate Plan that provides for the special person in their life. The consequence of not planning correctly can be devastating. If my dear client had not planned for her son correctly, her house would have been sold, and her money used to pay for her son's medical care, food, and shelter. For the son, this would have meant losing everything he loved, his home, his friends, his comic books and videos.

If you have a child with a disability, and he or she receives money from a Settlement, an Inheritance or gift, these funds can quickly disqualify the child (or adult) from public benefits. It is important to talk to an attorney who understands the benefit programs specially designed for children and adults with disabilities.

Part Nine

What happens if you lose your mind?

No one really loses their mind, but as you age your odds of succumbing to Alzheimer's or a related dementia increase, as do your chances of a stroke. These conditions can leave you vulnerable to abuse, losing valuable assets and to death, due to your neglect of yourself.

Unfortunately few people think about the possibility that they will become mentally incapacitated. We worry about losing our minds when we can't find out keys, or lose our wallet or purse, and losing things is a sign that your mind is going, but most often it is just inattention to detail. Mental incapacity can be obvious as it was in my mother in-laws situation where she literally forgot that her husband had gone to the hospital, and spent the night going from her bedroom to the kitchen and back because when he wasn't found in one room he must be in the other. This is what short term memory loss looks like. Short term memory loss comes with constantly repeating stories and questions, forgetting to eat, forgetting to pay bills and an inability to care for you.

There is a more subtle and insidious form of mental incapacity, which is a loss of judgment. Those who suffer from this will believe the scam artists. They will be sure that if they give the nice person some money it will be used to pay taxes on the money they won in a lottery, or they will buy a product that does not exist (like a phony oil well). A person can lose their ability to make logical decisions and have their memory intact making it difficult for family and friends to get them help, because this form of mental incapacity is not as well documented or as easily tested as the dementias that come with short term memory loss.

Dealing with a loved one who is mentally incapacitated is certainly one of the most difficult experiences of a lifetime. Whenever possible, we work with our clients to avoid the confrontational and often family-dividing legal remedy known as conservatorship.

Avoiding conservatorship issues should be one of your greatest motivators to see us for an comprehensive estate plan; so that in the event that you ever become incapacitated, no loved one will be faced with an adversarial court proceeding to have you declared incompetent.

A court-appointed conservatorship is a protective arrangement established by the legal system on behalf of a mentally incapacitated individual. Most frequently, conservatorships are established on behalf of older adults who have lost mental capacity due to senile dementia, major strokes, severe mental illness, or other conditions.

The Conservator of the person is in charge of making personal and medical decisions on behalf of a mentally incapacitated individual. The Conservator of the property is in charge of making financial decisions on behalf of such an individual. It is important to note that one person can serve as both Conservator of the person and of the property

I often help families establish conservatorships when an individual has lost mental capacity and no one can lawfully act for him/her. This is a painful process. A Conservatorship can often be avoided by Estate Planning that goes beyond planning for what happens when you die, but actually considers the possibility of mental incapacity (that you might lose your mind before you die).

If you don't have an Advance Health Care Directive, or Financial Power of Attorney; the doctors, bankers, and insurance agents who know you will not be able to legally allow your family to help you with the decisions you need to make. If you lose your ability to think logically and give the power to handle your finances to someone who uses it to steal from you or place you in a facility where you cannot leave; someone who is trustworthy will need to go to Court and establish a Conservatorship to protect you.

I cannot over-emphasize the importance of creating a plan where you have people you trust in charge of your legal, financial and healthcare decisions if you become mentally incapacitated. Bad people have a radar that enables them to find people having problems with their ability to think straight, if the people you trust have not been given permission to help you before this occurs, you may become a victim, and getting money back from bad guys is never easy. This is why Elder Law Attorneys like myself spend so much time planning for "What happens if you don't die?".

Part Ten

What is a Power of Attorney for Finances, Why do I need it?

A durable power of attorney for property management is a written instrument by which one person called the "principal" authorizes another person called the "attorney in fact" to act as the principal's agent, notwithstanding the principal's subsequent incapacity. The document can give the attorney in fact the authority to make decisions concerning the principals' real property, investments, cash, bank accounts, and trust. The durable power of attorney can be very broad, giving the attorney in fact power over all of the principal's assets, or narrow, giving the attorney in fact authority in fact power over specific assets.

If you become incapacitated, someone will need to manage your assets. If you become incapacitated, the court will be required to appoint a conservator to manage your assets, unless, a written document like a trust or durable power of attorney for property management authorizes someone to make decisions for you regarding each of your assets. If you have a living trust, the successor trustee can manage all the assets held by the trust, but he or she cannot manage any asset that was not transferred into the trust. This is yet another reason a trust must be kept current.

There are two kinds of power of attorney: general and special. A general durable power of attorney enables the attorney in fact to act on behalf of the principal with respect to all matters. A person who believes he or she will shortly be unable to handle his or her own affairs because of a medical condition such as Alzheimer's disease, should execute a durable power of attorney for property management as promptly as possible, so that their competency to do so is not questioned. If the power of attorney gives the attorney in fact only limited authority, it is "special", and the attorney in fact has only the authority granted in the document.

A Power of Attorney can become effective at a date later than the date it is signed. A springing power of attorney is a durable power of attorney that only becomes effective when a certain specified event occurs. The majority of this type of Durable Power of attorney becomes effective only after the principal becomes incapacitated, although another event or contingency can be specified. There are several difficulties with this type of power of attorney. First they are not authorized in some states. Second they are viewed with more mistrust than a traditional durable power of attorney. Third, there is difficulty in determining whether the "triggering" event has occurred, even though California law authorizes the principle to designate a person whose written declaration under penalty of perjury determines conclusively that the specified event has occurred.

A spouse is often the best candidate, to be the Attorney in Fact. However, if a spouse is unsophisticated in handling business matters, or is too ill to handle the task, a third party maybe a better choice. If your spouse is unable, or unwilling, (or you are not married), you may choose anyone to serve as your attorney in fact. In choosing this person, you MUST keep in mind that this person must be trustworthy. **A DURABLE POWER OF ATTORNEY FOR PROPERTY MANAGEMENT IS THE EQUIVALENT OF A BLANK CHECK.** If the person you choose as your agent is not a family member, you should consider a provision in the document that provides for them to be compensated.

A California Uniform Statutory Form Power of Attorney is available at most stationary and office supply forms. If the form is completed by you alone or at the suggestion of a friend of family member you may give too much Power to the wrong person or cause adverse tax consequences. A Power of Attorney is NOT just a form, it is a document that entrusts someone with all your money. It is a blessing in the right hands, and a curse in the wrong hands. It can be used to take all your money. An attorney should always be consulted before signing a Power of Attorney, and the Attorney should make sure that you understand the document and that you are the person who will benefit from giving this power away.

Part Eleven

Health Care Decisions, how can someone help.

I frequently hear concerns from clients, colleagues and friends that they don't want to live for months hooked up to machines, yet they also want the best medical care if there is hope of recovery, and a few more years on earth. As illness or age increase the greatest concern is that CPR will be used, and that life will be prolonged.

I am providing these materials to assist you in meeting the legal requirements to make your wishes known; and to provide you with the documents you need to insure that medical personnel will follow your wishes.

The first document you need to know about is an ADVANCE HEALTH CARE DIRECTIVE.

What is an Advance Health Care Directive?

An "Advance Health Care Directive" is the form which under California law allows you to appoint another person to be your health care "agent". This person will have the legal authority to make decisions about your medical care if you become unable to make these decisions for yourself. An "Advance Health Care Directive" allows you to write down your health care wishes, and your doctor and your agent must follow your lawful instructions.

An "Advance Health Care Directive" is highly recommended. In today's medical environment, doctors are very reluctant to listen to any family member who does not have written authority to act on your behalf. Family members who have a written document with your desires on it have both the legal authority to act, and confidence in acting because your wishes are written for them.

Do I need a "living will"?

The term "living will" was the general term which encompassed the Natural Death Act Declaration and other documents which allowed a person to state that they did not desire life sustaining treatment if they are terminally ill or permanently unconscious. An "Advance Heath Care Directive" is now the legally recognized format for a "living will"; it replaces the Natural Death Act Declaration, AND allows you to state your desires about your health care in any situation which you are unable to make your own decisions.

You will not need any additional documents; the "Advance Health Care Directive" contains a statement regarding your wishes about life-sustaining treatment.

What if I already have a "Durable Power of Attorney or Natural Death Act Declaration?

If you have a Durable Power of Attorney for Health Care executed before 1992; it has expired, and should be replaced. All other valid Durable Powers of Attorney and Natural Death Act Declarations remain valid.

The new "Advance Health Care Directive" gives you more flexibility, and by combining the designation of your agent with the statements regarding life-sustaining treatment it makes it simpler for your agent to act. At a minimum you should review your existent Durable Power of Attorney for Health Care or Natural Death Act Declaration to make sure it has not expired and that it still accurately reflects your wishes.

What are the legal requirements for completing an Advance health Care directive?

Any California resident who is at least eighteen (18) years old (or is an emancipated minor), of sound mind, and acting of his or her own free will can complete a valid Advance Health care Directive.

The document may be acknowledged before a notary public in California or two adult witnesses who are not appointed as your health care agents. These witnesses cannot be a health care provider or an employee of a health care provider, or an operator or an employee of a care facility for the elderly.

If a person is in a skilled nursing facility the document must be witnessed by an Ombudsman, and the telephone number of the Ombudsman must be posted at the facility.

Who should I appoint?

You can appoint any adult except your doctor, or a person who operates a facility (board and care home, residential care facility, or nursing home). However, they can be appointed if that person is related to you by blood, marriage or adoption, or is your co-worker.

The person you select should be someone you trust, and someone who has the ability to speak up for you. You should select someone who understands your wishes, and who is willing to accept this responsibility.

You may select one or more agents, who should be listed to act one at a time.

How much authority will my health care agent have?

Your agent has legal authority to speak for you in all health care matters. Health care professionals will look to your agent for decisions rather than your next of kin or any other persons. Your agent will be able to accept or refuse medical treatment, have access to your medical records, and make decisions about donating your organs, authorizing an autopsy, and disposing of your body should you die. The agent may not legally authorize convulsive treatment, psycho-surgery, sterilization, abortion or placement in a mental health treatment facility.

If you do not want your agent to have all these powers, you can write a statement in the Advance Health Care Directive form limiting your agent's authority. Your agent must make decisions consistent with any instructions you have written in the Advance Health Care Directive form.

What if I change my mind after completing and Advance Health Care Directive?

You can revoke or change an Advance Health Care Directive at any time. To revoke the entire form, including the appointment of your agent, you must inform all health care providers who have a copy of the of Advance Health care Directive in writing, and complete a new Advance Health Care Directive which should state that the previous directive was revoked.

How will emergency personnel (such as paramedics) find my Advance Health Care Directive form in the event of an emergency?

You need to be sure that the Advance health Care Directive is kept in an obvious place, and that your agent has a copy. If you specifically do not want to be

Resuscitated, a Do not Resuscitate form is also included with this information. To be effective the form must be signed by your physician. You should order a medic alert bracelet so that paramedics know immediately your wishes. Paramedics rarely look at wallets.

Is an Advance Health Care Directive valid in other States?

If you spend a lot of time in another state you should consult lawyer in that State, if you are traveling, most states will recognize an Advance Health Care directive that is executed legally in another State, but they are not required by law to honor it.

A GUIDE TO DETAILING YOUR WISHES

In order to assist you in making these decisions, I have developed some question which will help you to describe how you feel.

Describe what medical care if any you want to receive if you were in a coma, and your life expectancy was not certain?

How do you feel about being fed by a tube, when you no longer can eat?

If you are permanently unable to recognize and communicate with people, and you an able to feel pain, and are aware of your surroundings, how much medical care would you want? If you contracted an illness (such as pneumonia, urinary tract infection, etc.) that could be cured or reversed would you want care to cure the illness?

If you have a disease or condition that cannot be cured, and you are told that you will die within six months, what kind of medical care do you want? If you contracted an illness (such as pneumonia, urinary tract infection, etc.) that could be cured or reversed would you want care to cure the illness?

Are there any medical conditions your family should know about?

Do you have any special requests regarding burial, or your funeral service?

WHAT WOULD YOU WANT YOUR FAMILY TO DO IF YOU WERE LIKE TERRI SCHIAVO?

Most of you have heard about and seen Terri Schiavo. For those of us who don't remember, Teri suffered a heart attack, and after heroic measures to save her, she was in a coma described as a persistent vegetative state. She woke up, and appeared to be able to see and hear. Everyone had an opinion, and it was heart wrenching to watch as her husband and parents fought over her fate. No one really knows what Terri Schiavo really wanted, because she never wrote it down. A conservative republican Judge found the evidence presented by her husband that she would not want to be artificially kept alive clear and convincing, and the power to make the decision was given to her husband. Terri Schiavo was being kept alive through the artificial administration of food and hydration. She was a shy woman who never would have wanted to have her life and death the center of world attention. No one I know would want such a private matter made into such a public spectacle. After the Court allowed her husband to remove the artificial food and hydration, and an autopsy was performed the coroner found that her brain was like Jell-O and that she could not see and that the waking was a reflex, and that she only appeared to know that someone was nearby.

As an elder law attorney, I understand how important it is to put in writing what you would want done if you were terminally ill, in a coma, or persistent vegetative state. I advise clients on their options, and draft specific instructions for their family. You are never too young to think about what you would want your family to do if a tragedy occurred and decisions needed to be made. If your family must decide for you they need to know what you want, I can prepare you to have that talk with your family. If you have an advance healthcare documents prepared your family can have peace of mind that they honored your wishes, they will have in writing your philosophy of death and dying. Most people have strong opinions on this subject; many have deeply held religious convictions. I don't "just" provide my clients with Advance Healthcare Directives ("Living Wills"), I also provide them with the advice and information they need to provide direction to their family when the time comes and their family must decide what to do when their loved one is in the hospital and not able to communicate their desires

Part Twelve

Paying for Nursing Home Care

MEDI-CAL PLANNING

Many courts have commented that federal Medicaid laws are the most complicated law that have ever been promulgated by Congress with the exception of the Internal Revenue Code. In California, the Medicaid program is called Medi-Cal, and there are many special laws, rules, regulations and interpretations which increase the confusion.

Achieving Medi-Cal eligibility can even challenge attorneys who practice in this area every day. There are two major categories of Medi-Cal benefits, one pays for medical care for the truly indigent, and the other pays for Skilled Nursing Care in a facility licensed to provide for this level of care, i.e. a nursing home. Providing for care and preserving assets require careful planning, and a clear focus that we must always make sure we have the best interests of the person facing the need for care as our primary focus.

When you are looking for help paying for Long Term Care, the State will also be looking at all of your gifts and transfers. The rules are complicated and are almost always in a state of flux. Information on the internet is typically not current, and also often less that accurate. There is much information on my elder law website www.ElderLawMom.com; I spend hundreds of hours every year in seminars, conferences and personal study analyzing and understanding all the rules; so I can properly advise clients on those gifts that will count and cause problems with qualification; and so I can help them make gifts that will not create a nightmare of disqualification.

For most of us, our biggest asset is our home. Our home has perhaps both our largest financial asset and our greatest sentimental value. Most people want our home to go to our children when we pass, we certainly don't want our home or our assets to go to the State of California. With proper planning, a home can be protected and you need not lose your home to pay for care.

The State of California does everything it can to recover the money from the estates of the people it has spent on their nursing home care; it is ruthless and relentless in this recovery pursuit. When your family plans to preserve assets while having the State of California through Medi-Cal pay for your loved one's skilled nursing care; you must have as part of your planning strategy prevention of the State of California getting repayment from you, their heirs. The rules for avoiding recovery are far more complex than the rules for qualifying for Medi-Cal. Therefore, it is important to seek the advice of a person who is keeping up to date on the myriads of rules and regulations being promulgated by the State.

If you as a loved one are facing the need for care outside the home, you should seek advice from a qualified Elder Law Attorney as soon as you find out that care in the home is no longer an option. The sooner you seek advice the better; early planning gives you the most possible choices available. I am available to assist you with Medi-Cal Planning. For help call 855-ELDER77 or (855)353-3777 or go to www.ElderLawMom.com.

Part Thirteen

VETERAN'S BENEFITS, ANNUTIES, AND ACCREDITATION

Accreditation

There are many organizations implying they have an association with the Veterans Administration, as they use "Veteran's" or "Veteran" in their name. They offer to qualify people to the Veteran's benefit for free. The reason they are offering to work for free is the law prohibits charging for or assisting with applications for Veteran's benefits. The problem is: unless they are accredited; they are also prohibited from providing education, or assisting with Veteran's Benefits.

According to the Veterans Administration, Accreditation means the authority granted by VA to assist claimants in the preparation, presentation, and prosecution of claims for benefits. 38 C.F.R. § 14.627(a). Unaccredited individuals may provide other services to veterans so long as they do not assist in the preparation, presentation, and prosecution of claims for benefits. The Veteran's Administration **includes** education in that definition. The Veteran's Administration is concerned about the sale of annuities, as often annuities are sold in circumstances that constitute elder abuse. I have researched several people giving presentations in this area, so far not one of them is listed as accredited. A list of accredited individuals is located at www.va.gov.

It would appear that at this point of publication (January 2013), the Veteran's Administration does not restrict the use of annuities; however, Medi-Cal does. Unfortunately, if a person needs skilled care, the annuity sold to qualify the person for Veteran's Benefits will disqualify them for Medi-Cal.

Part Fourteen

Veteran's Benefits to Pay for Care

What Are Aid and Attendance Benefits?
Aid and Attendance is a benefit paid by Veterans Affairs (VA) to veterans, veteran spouses or surviving spouses. It is paid in *addition* to a veteran's basic pension. The benefit may not be paid without eligibility to a VA basic pension. Aid and Attendance is for applicants who need financial help for in–home care, or to pay for an assisted living facility or a nursing home. It is a non–service connected disability benefit, meaning the disability does not have to be a result of service. You cannot receive non–service and service–connected compensation at the same time.

Aid and Attendance benefits are paid to those applicants who:

- Are eligible for a VA pension
- Meet service requirements
- Meet certain disability requirements
- Meet income and asset limitations

Basic Eligibility for VA Pension

1. Be a veteran who served at least 90 days of active duty or the surviving spouse of a wartime veteran (married at the time of veteran's death)
2. At least one day of active duty had to be during wartime:
   - WWII – 12/07/1941 to 07/25/1947
   - Korea – 06/27/1950 to 12/31/1955
   - Vietnam – 08/05/1964 to 05/07/1975
   (02/28/1961-05/07/1975 if in Vietnam proper)
3. Does not need to have been in combat
4. Discharged other than dishonorably
   - Honorable discharge
   - Discharge under honorable conditions
   - General Discharge
   - Bad conduct discharge, Discharge under other than honorable conditions, or Undesirable discharge <u>may</u> still be eligible after a "character of service determination" hearing

5. Income limits:
   All unreimbursed medical expenses are deducted from income including Assisted Living if you need a "protective environment" and need assistance with activities of daily living.
6. Net worth:
   Less than $80,000; however, the Veteran's Administration will adjust downward for age, so as you age the amount of net worth you can retain is less.
7. Service Connected Disability:
   The Veteran's administration has determined that certain conditions are connected to military service attached is the most recent chart. For Vietnam Veterans some new conditions are being added, if a spouse died from certain diseases the spouse is entitled to Service Connected Benefits. If your medical condition (or your deceased spouse had the condition) you are entitled to benefits regardless of assets or income.
8. CHAMPVA and Tricare: These are medical insurance benefits which may be available. Retired Veterans and their spouse or widow(er)

are eligible for Tricare which covers medications, and some medical supplies. CHAMPVA provides medical coverage and medications to Veterans and spouses.

9. Special Benefits: Dependent children and parents may be entitled to benefits.

IT IS ILLEGAL FOR ANYONE TO CHARGE YOU, YOUR SPOUSE, YOUR CHILDREN, YOUR GRANDCHILDREN, ANY ONE YOU PAY FOR CARE, OR ANYONE WHO COULD RECEIVE MONEY FROM YOUR ESTATE TO:

Prepare, Present or Prosecute a claim on behalf of a Veteran 8 CFR 14.629. Further anyone preparing, presenting or prosecuting claims **must** be accredited by the Veteran's Administration.

AARP warns of many scams targeting Veterans using Veterans Benefits as a lure to sell annuities. (Scam Alert: Taking Aim at Old Soldiers);

TO FIND OUT IF SOME ONE IS ACCREDITED GO TO http://www.va.gov/ogc/apps/accreditation/index.asp

Part Fifteen

Nine Common And Costly Estate Planning Mistakes

Mistakes are part of life. Some mistakes can be life threatening. Fortunately some mistakes can be avoided or eliminated by thinking ahead; So it is with estate planning mistakes. This is a warning about the most common mistakes; the list is **not** exclusive.

1. Procrastination: Most people have no plan at all. Who wants to face the possibility of their future incapacity and the certainty of their death? It is an ugly proposition. Nevertheless, only you can make your estate plan a top priority. Otherwise you expose yourself, your loved ones and your hard-earned assets to probate and avoidable death taxes. Take time to carefully think through, implement and then update your estate plan. You and your loved ones will be glad you did.

2. Not planning for Incapacity: Too many people think estate planning relates to distributing assets after death. Total estate planning begins with planning for your own incapacity (the day when your mind fails). Adults are required to make their own personal, health care and financial decisions. If you have not given someone permission to make these decisions for you, a probate judge will be required to appoint someone who will make the decisions for you. The process of having a court name someone for you is painful and extremely expensive.

3. No back-up Parents: Most parents consider their children to be their most valuable assets. These parents often devote considerable time and treasure to providing educations, activities and religious training for their children. Incredibly, these same parents typically fail to legally appoint guardians for their minor children in the event both parents die. When back up parents are not selected in writing prior to death great hardship and even custody battles can ensue between well-meaning friends or relatives.

4. Winding up in Probate Court: Many people overlook simple steps to ensure that their estate -or at least a big chunk of it –avoids being processed through probate court. Probate proceedings can drag on for months or even years and can eat up to 5 percent or more of an estate's value. Contact and consult with an Estate Planning Attorney in order to avoid probate, and avoid risks created by techniques such as joint tenancy which expose you to the possibility that the person you add to title on your property or bank account will take your assets.

5. No Inheritance Protection: No one values a dollar like the person who earned it. If you do not incorporate *inheritance protection* into your estate planning, your hard-earned assets could be squandered by your surviving spouse's new spouse, your or their children or grandchildren, or lost to heir divorces, lawsuits or bankruptcies. Enough said.

6. Keeping Poor Records: One of the biggest mistakes people make is not regularly updating their estate plans. Every two or three years, blow the dust off your estate plan and go through it. When estate plans are old, children are more likely to argue about what dad or mom really intended, which can cause horrible fights and destruction of family relationships. Sometimes an out of date estate plan names people who are no longer alive, or worse, fail to name new members of the family.

7. No Estate Tax Planning: Many people think the Estate Tax cannot possibly apply to them. It is common for people to be surprised at how much they actually own after they make a list of all their assets including life insurance. You may not think your estate is big enough or that estate taxes will go away but if you guess wrong, and you do not plan to avoid estate taxes, the IRS could assess your heirs hundreds of thousands of dollars, much of which could have been avoided.

8. Being Disorganized: It is not uncommon for a family struck with grief, or finally admitting mom or dad cannot handle their personal business; to find they have no idea of what a loved one owns, where their Will or Trust is, or where the safety deposit box or key is. When files are in a shambles, relatives can spend weeks or months tracking down assets. Leaving a disorganized estate can also dramatically inflate legal bills after a death, regardless of the size of the estate.

9. Failing to make Special Plans for Disabled Children: Once a disabled child becomes an adult, they will receive essential government benefits. If they receive an inheritance they can be disqualified from receiving these benefits. A "special Needs Trust" can be set up as part of your estate plan to make sure that they can receive their benefits while a trustee can insure that they receive the things that make them comfortable and happy. If you leave a disabled child's inheritance to their brother's and sister's, the disabled child's inheritance is not protected. Planning ahead will give your disabled child a good life even when you are gone.

"An Ounce of Prevention is worth a Pound of Cure"

Part Sixteen

"Now What"

We started with "What If". You have been presented with admittedly a daunting amount of information and numbers. Perhaps you are feeling overwhelmed, I know my husband and brother in law did as they dealt with the tragic discovery of their mother starting on the road of Alzheimer's. Perhaps you now have many more questions than answers. That is where I come into the picture. I am here to help you through this process. I am sure you have found this book useful, but I also know that there is nothing like talking face to face. Since I know you want to plan for your family so you are prepared for all the "What if's" of life and death, please don't hesitate to give me a call at (855) ELDER77 or (855)353-3777. I enjoy helping people and guiding them as they make the decisions necessary to make sure that families are prepared for life, dementia, disability, disease, as well as death. I guarantee that I will provide you with the most current legal solutions for your situation.

This book was written by

Martha Jo Geisler Patterson, J.D., CELA
certified by the National Elder Law Foundation

Published by Geisler Patterson Law

Mailing Address
P.O. Box 33968
Granada Hills, CA 91394

Offices in Burbank and Woodland HillsCalifornia

Phone: 855 ELDER-77 or 855.353.3777

Email: mjplawmom@gmail.com

And on the web at: www.ElderLawMom.com

www.ingramcontent.com/pod-product-compliance
Lightning Source LLC
Chambersburg PA
CBHW060420190526
45169CB00002B/983